How To Draw
Fairies

HOW TO DRAW

Fairies

Artist and author
Samantha Chaffey

Contents

Materials

To START DRAWING FAIRIES, ALL YOU NEED IS A PENCIL AND PAPER. YOU CAN ALSO EXPERIMENT WITH LOTS OF DIFFERENT MATERIALS.

Different materials

Try colouring your fairies using paints and pastels. You could even use two different materials in the same picture.

Coloured pencils

Sharp and blunt pencils create different effects. You can use delicate strokes for highlights or press hard on your paper for dark areas.

Felt-tip pens

Using felt-tip pens will make your picture look like a cartoon, especially if you outline it with a black felt-tip pen.

Glitter pens

Fairies love sparkle! You could use glitter pens to decorate your pictures.

Collage

Instead of colouring your fairies, you could stick on coloured paper. Try using scraps of material for the clothes or wool for the hair.

Paper

Drawing on different types of paper can change the look of your picture. Experiment using different colours and textures.

5

Figures

PRACTISE DRAWING A BASIC FIGURE. FOLLOW THESE STAGES TO BUILD A BODY, BIT BY BIT.

① Draw the basic head and body. Guidelines will help you shape the body and position the facial features.

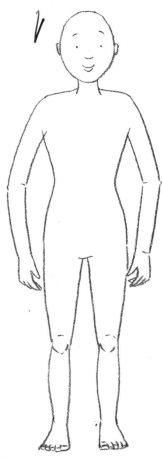

Head

Neck

Torso

How to do draw basic figures

② Add positional lines for the arms and legs. You can use small circles to help you place the joints, such as the knees and elbows.

③ Use the guidelines to shape the body, arms and legs. Add the facial features and rough shapes for the hands and feet.

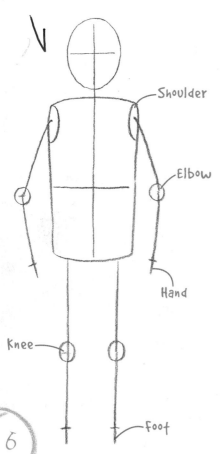

Shoulder

Elbow

Hand

Knee

Foot

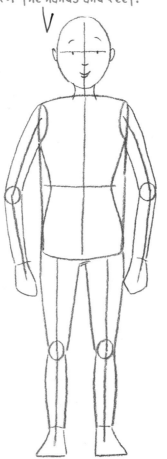

④ Now you can erase the guidelines and add detail to the hands and feet.

Different poses

The proportions of a figure will change if they are in different positions. Parts of the body will look smaller and other parts will look bigger.

From this angle, the Summer fairy's body and legs look longer.

The Summer fairy is lying on her front. Her body and legs look short, but her head and shoulders look big. This is because they are closer to you.

The Buttercup fairy is flying towards you. Her feet look tiny as they are far away. The shape of the skirt of her dress also looks different from this angle.

From the side, the Buttercup fairy looks more in proportion.

Features

LOOK AROUND YOU AND SEE HOW DIFFERENT EVERYONE SEEMS TO BE, EVEN THOUGH THEIR FEATURES ARE BASICALLY THE SAME. LITTLE DIFFERENCES MAKE BIG CHANGES TO FACES.

Making faces

Use a cross as a guideline to position facial features. Then you can add a variety of details to create characters.

LOOK IN THE MIRROR AND SEE HOW YOUR FACE CHANGES WHEN YOU SMILE OR FROWN. NOTICE WHAT HAPPENS TO YOUR EYEBROWS AND MOUTH.

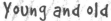

Young and old

Young faces usually have small features and rounded cheeks. Grey hair will make someone look older.

Expressions

A mouth can curve downwards to show a frown or upwards to form a smile. Eyebrows can help show surprise or anger.

Male and female

Men sometimes have beards and heavier features. Women have different hairstyles and more delicate features.

Hairstyles

There are lots of hairstyles to draw! You can change many things to give each fairy a unique look.

Add accessories
You could add flowers or jewels to your fairy's hair, or draw hair in plaits or pigtails.

Short, dark and straight
Use straight, smooth lines for sleek hair. Leave areas white to show shine.

Long, blonde and curly
Use wavy lines to show curls. Use a dark gold to show texture for blonde hair.

Hands and feet

To get used to drawing hands and feet, draw around your own on some paper.

1. Draw the basic hand shape first. It looks like a mitten.

2. Divide the hand shape into four fingers and a thumb.

1. Draw the basic shape of a foot. Add a cross to guide you in the direction it is facing.

2. Shape the foot and divide it to form toes. Remember that toes are different sizes.

Holding
Fingers bend around what they are holding. Look at your own hand holding objects to help you draw a fairy holding a wand.

9

Fashion

YOU CAN HAVE ENDLESS FUN DRAWING CLOTHES FOR YOUR FAIRIES. USE YOUR IMAGINATION AND SEE WHAT DESIGNS YOU CAN CREATE.

Change trousers and a top by adding colours and patterns

Add a belt to define the waist

Drawing clothes

Draw the shape and position of the body first, then add the clothes.

LOOK THROUGH YOUR HOUSE AND SEE HOW MANY THINGS HAVE PATTERNS ON THEM. THEY MAY GIVE YOU LOTS OF NEW IDEAS FOR FAIRY CLOTHES.

Draw the rough shape of the crown to guide you

Use the shape of the body to form the waist

Draw large bell shapes for dresses and skirts

Decorating clothes

Once you've decided on the shape of your fairy's outfit, you can change how it looks by adding detail to the material it is made from or by drawing a pattern.

Dress of leaves

Add texture to leaves by drawing lines for the veins. Shade areas darker to show the shadow from the top leaves.

Dress of petals

Use the shape of petals to form the skirt of the dress. Shade areas darker where petals overlap or join the waistband.

Decorate with stars

Draw star shapes all over the material. Then colour the background, leaving the stars white.

Stripy tights

Shoes

Boots

Wellies

Spotty tights

Tights and shoes
Have fun decorating your fairy's tights with spots or stripes. You could add bows, buckles or flowers to their shoes or boots.

LOOK AT YOUR OWN CLOTHES. SEE HOW THEY FIT AND WHERE THEY CREASE WHEN YOU MOVE. ALSO HAVE A LOOK AT WHAT THEY ARE MADE FROM.

Adding extras
You don't have to stop at clothes and shoes. You could add jewellery, a hat or a bag to match your fairy's outfit.

Bag
Some fairies carry bags to help them do their jobs. Think about what size and shape bag your fairy needs.

Tiara
Use the shape of your fairy's head to add a tiara. You could also add a necklace, bracelet or earrings.

Hat
This fairy is wearing a warm, winter hat, but you could draw a summer hat with flowers on.

Movement

FAIRIES ARE ALWAYS BUSY! AS WELL AS DRAWING THEM STANDING OR SITTING STILL, YOU WILL WANT TO DRAW THEM MOVING AND DOING EXCITING THINGS.

Creating movement

Decide which direction your fairy is moving, then draw a line across your paper in the same direction. You can use this as a guideline to help you draw wavy hair and movement lines.

This fairy is skating forwards, so add little lines to show movement behind her

The Spring cleaning fairy is brushing dust everywhere, so the movement lines go in all directions

Flying or standing

Fairies in the same position can be flying or standing still. Add a line of ground that your fairy is flying above or standing on.

You can also add movement lines behind your fairy's wings to show that she is flying

If your fairy is standing still, make sure that she is touching the ground beneath her

12

Fairy scenes

ONCE YOU FEEL CONFIDENT DRAWING FAIRY CHARACTERS, YOU CAN BEGIN TO ADD BACKGROUND DETAILS. TRY PUTTING YOUR FAIRIES IN A SCENE AND TELLING A STORY.

TAKE YOUR SKETCHBOOK TO THE GARDEN OR PARK AND PRACTISE DRAWING WHAT YOU SEE.

Daytime scene

These fairies are sitting in a garden enjoying a chat and a cool drink.

You can show the size of your fairies by the size of the objects around them. These fairies are very small, as the toadstools and flowers are as big as them

Night-time scene

These two fairies are discussing their day before they go to sleep.

At night-time, shadows are cast by objects. Notice that the objects and surfaces near the lamp are lighter than those further away

13

Tooth Fairy

1

Draw an oval for the head, a rounded square for the torso and a large, bell shape for the skirt of the dress.

Draw a cross as a guide to position the eyes, nose and mouth

This side of the body is more rounded

The shapes overlap slightly

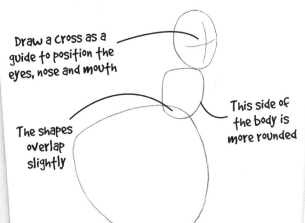

2

Add petal-shaped wings. Use guidelines to draw the arms and add rough shapes for the hands.

Draw a flattened circle for the neckline and add the neck

Place a small circle for the shoulder

Guidelines will help you position the legs

Begin to draw the legs and feet

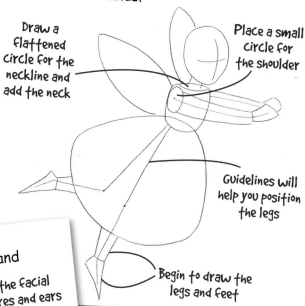

3

Begin to shape the arms, legs and skirt of the dress.

Add the facial features and ears

Draw the bag she collects the teeth in

Draw in the hands holding the tooth

Shape the feet

The Tooth Fairy comes at night to collect children's baby teeth!

4 Rub out the guidelines and start to add the details.

The hair is made up of curved lines with flicks at the ends

Begin to shade the face

Add lines to show movement

You can decorate her bag

Start to add lines for the material of the skirt of the dress

To show that your fairy is flying, add sweeping lines going the opposite way to the direction your fairy is facing.

5 Use a soft, coloured pencil to colour the skin. This will make it look smooth. Colour your fairy's dress, tights, wings and bag in pinks and blues. Use darker shades to outline the detail in her clothes and wings.

Use yellow to show how magic and sparkle glows!

Fairy Godmother

1
Draw a small circle on top of two large, squashed circles. The shapes are all overlapping.

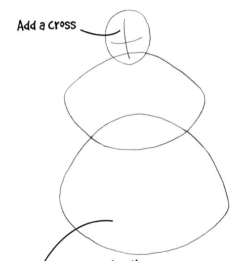

Add a cross

Make this shape slightly bigger than the one above it

Make your picture tell a story. Add a pumpkin and a mouse to show what your fairy godmother is casting a spell on.

2
Add petal-shaped wings and a small circle on the top of the head.

Hair is up in a bun

A triangle will help you to draw her cape

Draw the guidelines for the arms

Rounded shapes for the hands

Add guidelines to help you position the feet

The Fairy Godmother is busy helping to make wishes come true!

3 Add the facial features and detail to the hair. Shape the hands, arms and clothes.

Use triangle shapes to form a bow

Add a wand

Draw the shoes and rub out your guidelines

4 You can erase all the guidelines and add all the fun details, such as the stars on her skirt.

Add swirly lines to show magic

Lines make creases where she is holding her skirt

Start to add shading

5 Colour your fairy in. You could use different colours for the skirt and cape. Use darker shades in areas that are further away, such as the edges of the skirt and cape, and to add detail to creases and folds in the fabric.

You can colour the wand black and white, just like a magician's!

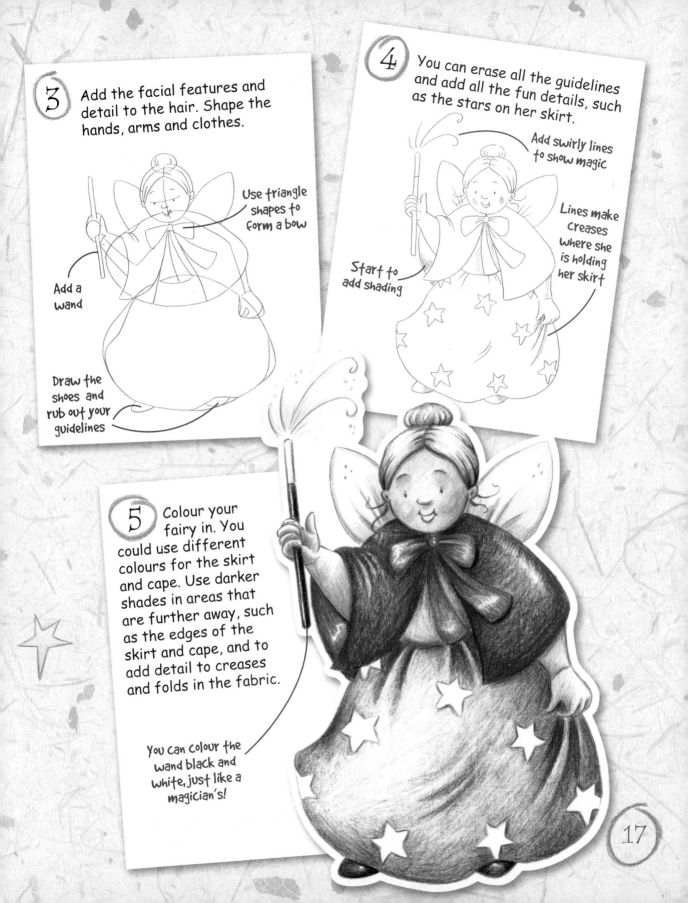

Christmas Fairy

1
Draw an oval for the head and a small, squashed square for the torso. Add a large, bell shape for the skirt of the dress.

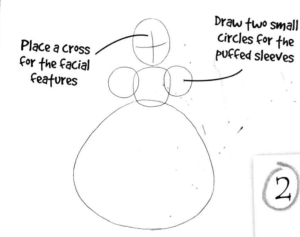

Place a cross for the facial features

Draw two small circles for the puffed sleeves

To add texture and shape to clothes, use darker shading where fabric joins or creases. Leave areas lighter for highlights.

2
Add four petal shapes for the wings. You can draw guidelines to help you position the feet.

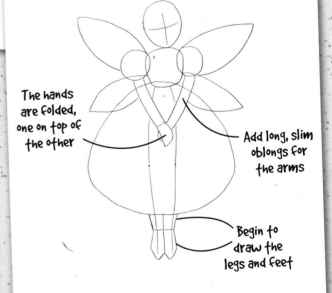

The hands are folded, one on top of the other

Add long, slim oblongs for the arms

Begin to draw the legs and feet

This special fairy has the important job of making the Christmas tree look dazzling!

3 Add the facial features, ears and neck. Begin to shape the arms and hands.

Draw the neckline of her dress

Start to show wing detail

Add a sash at the waist

Begin to draw the wand

Wiggly lines will begin to create the frilly edge of the dress

4 Erase your guidelines and add detail to the dress and wings. Draw the hair and the shoes.

Use wavy lines for curly hair

Draw in the branches of the tree

Shape the wand and add a star at the end

Use lots of lines to show the tree's needles

5 Use different shades of green for the Christmas tree. Colour the fairy's dress and shoes in shades of red. The sash and underskirt should be green. Add red and green stripes to the tights. Colour the wings, hair and star of the wand in shades of yellow.

Use light green to colour the tree and then add detail with a dark green pencil

You could add baubles to the branches of your tree.

Fairy Prince

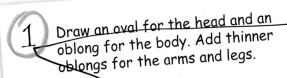

1 Draw an oval for the head and an oblong for the body. Add thinner oblongs for the arms and legs.

The arm shapes are curved

Place a cross

You can use guidelines to help you position the legs and feet

Draw two oblongs for the bent leg

Add rough shapes for the feet

2 Rounded shapes will help you form the hands. Add a guideline for his belt.

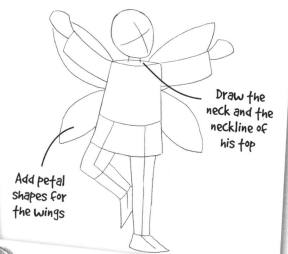

Draw the neck and the neckline of his top

Add petal shapes for the wings

3 Start to shape the arms and legs. Use your guidelines to shape the clothes.

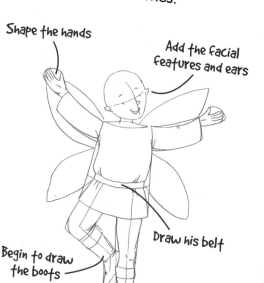

Shape the hands

Add the facial features and ears

Draw his belt

Begin to draw the boots

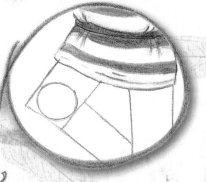

If you find it hard to draw bent legs or arms, add a circle to help you shape a knee or elbow.

4 Rub out your guidelines. Add the hat and draw some tufts of hair poking out.

Draw the acorns he is juggling and little lines to show their movement

Add details to the wings

Shade the belt

You could draw stripes or spots on his top

He is standing on grass

This cheeky fairy prince loves to juggle with whatever he can find while playing in the woods!

5 You can add freckles to your fairy's cheeks with an orange or light brown pencil. Use different shades of brown for the acorns and his hat and boots.

Use bright colours for his top and make his trousers a different colour

Toadstool Fairy

1 Draw a big, squashed oval with a rectangle below it for the toadstool.

When fairies need a rest, they find a comfortable toadstool to sit on and enjoy a nice, cool drink!

Draw an oval and add a cross

A small circle will help you place the arm and shoulder

Draw two overlapping, rounded shapes for the torso and skirt of the dress

2 Add the wings. Draw slim oblongs for the arms and legs. Use guidelines if you need help to position them.

Add the neck

Draw the cup she is holding

A mitten shape will help you draw the hand

Begin to draw the feet

3 Use the cross to help you draw the facial features. Add little lines to her wings and begin to shape her dress, arms, hands, legs and feet.

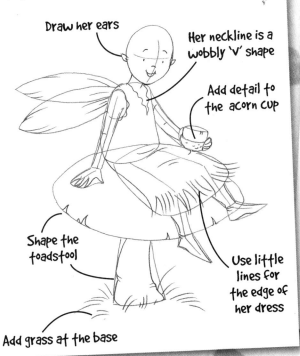

Draw her ears

Her neckline is a wobbly 'V' shape

Add detail to the acorn cup

Shape the toadstool

Use little lines for the edge of her dress

Add grass at the base

4 Add the hair and a flower behind her ear. Erase the guidelines and add the details. You can begin to add shading to her dress and the toadstool.

Add bubbles!

The toadstool is covered with spots

The tights could be stripy or spotty

5 Use a bright red to colour the toadstool, but leave the spots white. Outline the spots with a dark red pencil. Use different tones of a single colour to add texture and shade to the fairy's dress.

Colour the grass shades of green

Buttercup Fairy

The Buttercup Fairy is busy collecting buttercups to make special fairy butter!

1
Draw two small, overlapping ovals for the head and torso. Add one large circle for the skirt of the dress.

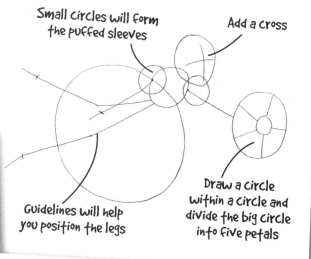

Small circles will form the puffed sleeves

Add a cross

Guidelines will help you position the legs

Draw a circle within a circle and divide the big circle into five petals

2
Begin to draw the arms and legs. Add the neck and neckline of the dress. You can start to shape the petals of the flower.

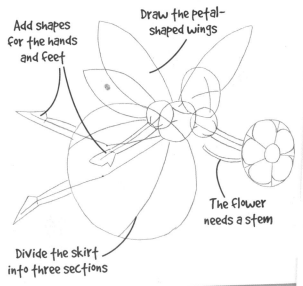

Add shapes for the hands and feet

Draw the petal-shaped wings

Divide the skirt into three sections

The flower needs a stem

3
Begin to shape the arms, hands, legs and feet. Use little, soft lines to shape and add texture to her dress and the flower.

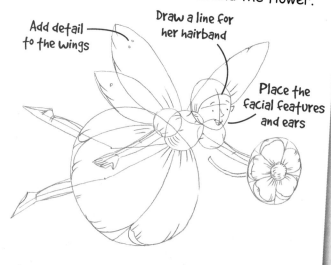

Add detail to the wings

Draw a line for her hairband

Place the facial features and ears

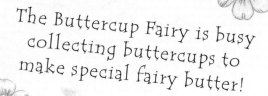

4 Now you can erase the guidelines. Start to draw the hair using lots of wiggly, wavy lines. Add a few strands of hair in front of the hairband too.

Use bright yellow for the buttercup. Then use little fine lines, in darker golds and browns, to shade from the centre of the flower.

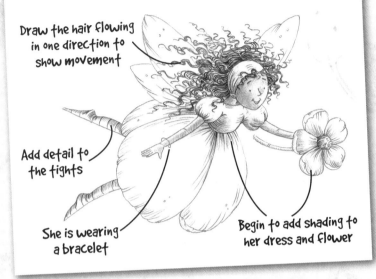

Draw the hair flowing in one direction to show movement

Add detail to the tights

She is wearing a bracelet

Begin to add shading to her dress and flower

5 Use yellows and oranges to colour her dress, tights, hairband, wings and flower. Colour the stem of the flower green. You can add movement lines to show that she is flying through the air.

Use black and brown for her hair, but remember to leave sections white to show texture and shine

Fairy Princess

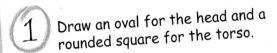

1

Draw an oval for the head and a rounded square for the torso.

The top layer of the dress is a squashed oval

Draw a cross to help you position the facial features

Add a bell shape for the lower layer of the dress

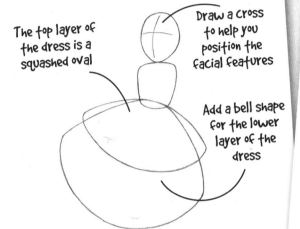

2

Use guidelines to position the arms and legs. Then you can add lines on either side to shape them.

Add petal-shaped wings

Rough shapes will help you draw the feet

Draw rough shapes for the hands

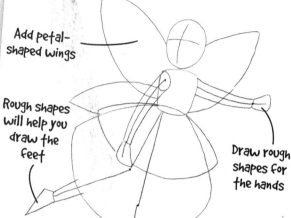

3

Add the facial features. Start to shape the petals of the dress, and the arms, hands, legs and feet.

Add the neck and neckline of the dress

Add a wand

Use little lines to add detail to the skirt of the dress

To create a wand, draw a star shape at the top of a thin stick. Add swirly lines, sparkly spots or little stars to create magic!

4 Rub out the guidelines and start to shade. Add fine lines to the wings.

Add a tiara

Use lots of curvy lines for the hair

You can draw stripes on the tights

The Fairy Princess loves to cast spells with her special wand!

5 For the skin, use soft, circular movements with a blunt pencil. Then use a dark brown pencil to outline and show detail. You can use different colours for the top and lower layer of her dress.

Add little lines to show that the tights are slightly wrinkled above the heel

Rose Fairy

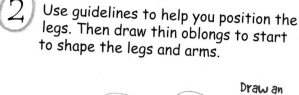

1

Draw a large circle for the skirt of the dress, with a small circle just inside for the torso.

Add round, petal shapes for the wings

Draw an oval for the head and place a cross

Another small circle will help you position the legs

2

Use guidelines to help you position the legs. Then draw thin oblongs to start to shape the legs and arms.

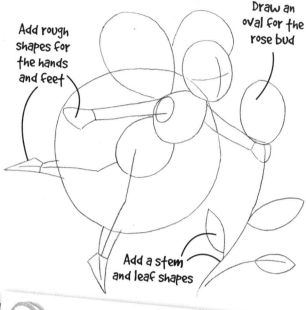

Add rough shapes for the hands and feet

Draw an oval for the rose bud

Add a stem and leaf shapes

3

Begin to shape her arms, hands, legs and feet. Add the facial features.

She is smelling the rose with her eyes closed

Draw the neck and neckline of the dress

Divide the dress into petals and start to shape the edges

Begin to add details to the rose

The Rose Fairy collects all the fallen rose petals to make perfume and rose petal tea!

Add texture and detail to the Rose fairy's dress with darker pinks and reds. Remember to leave light areas for highlights.

Rub out the guidelines. Add little lines to the edges of the wings and the petals of the dress.

Her hair is short

Shape the hands

Shape the rose bud

Add spots to the tights

Use pale pink for the rose bud and shades of green to colour the stem and leaves

5 Use soft strokes to show delicate petals. Colour using pale pink for the wings and highlights in the dress. Use darker shades of pink for areas of the dress and the tights. Colour the spots of the tights in dark pink.

Spring Cleaning Fairy

The Spring Cleaning Fairy is always busy and loves to make everything neat and tidy!

1 Draw an oval for the head. Add a cross to show where to place the facial features.

Draw the petal-shaped wings

Add a squashed square for the torso

The fourth wing is hidden behind the fairy's body

A bell shape will help you form the skirt of the dress

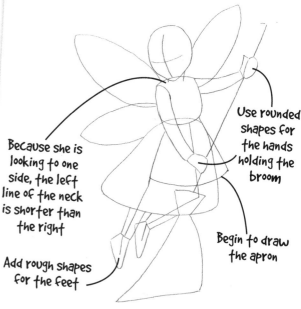

2 Draw guidelines to help you position the legs. Then add slim oblongs for the arms and legs. Begin to draw the shape of the broom.

Use rounded shapes for the hands holding the broom

Because she is looking to one side, the left line of the neck is shorter than the right

Add rough shapes for the feet

Begin to draw the apron

3 Shape the arms and legs. Draw pointed lines for the edge of the dress. Add thin lines to the wings.

Add the facial features

Shape the top of the dress

Start to draw the gloves and boots

Begin to add detail to the broom

4 Erase the guidelines. Add the hair and little details, such as the pocket on her apron and the bows.

The long hair is plaited

Add smudges of dirt with a pencil

Use little lines for the broom

Lines will show the dust flying up from the floor

5 Use browns to colour the broom. You could use a red pencil and draw vertical and horizontal lines on her apron, creating a pattern. Use blue to colour her dress and red to colour her wellies.

Use shades of brown to draw the floor that she is sweeping

Summer Fairy

The Summer Fairy has found a lily pad to rest on to cool her feet in the water!

1 Draw an oval for the head and a rounded, rectangle shape below it. Add a tilted oval on top of the head, with a tiny circle in the middle of it.

A small circle will help you position the arm

Add a cross

Start to draw the legs and arms with guidelines

Draw a large oval for the lily pad

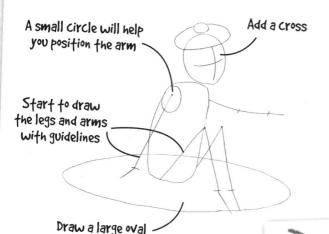

The eyebrows and mouth help to show if someone is happy, sad, surprised or angry...

2 Draw the wings. Begin to draw the arms, legs and feet. Add rough, mitten shapes for the hands.

You can draw circles where the legs bend to help you form the knees

Draw her neck and the neckline of her dress

This hand will be flat as it is resting on the lily pad

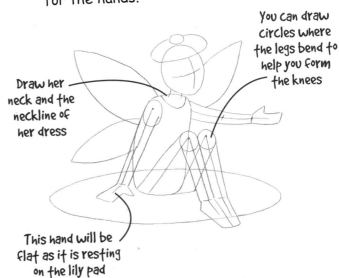

... Can you see how different the Summer Fairy looks when you change her eyebrows and mouth?

3 Start to draw her dress. You can only see part of it, as she is sitting with her legs bent. Add the facial features and ears.

Divide the oval into sections

Add a butterfly

Start to shape the lily pad

Begin to shape the hands and feet

Draw ripples in the water

4 Erase the guidelines. Use long lines for her hair. You could add a flower design to the dress. Draw little lines to add detail to the wings and for the ripples in the water.

Shape the petals and add little lines

Begin to shade down her body

Add details to the lily pad and butterfly

You can't see her toes because they are in the water

5 Use different shades of blue to show the water. Colour the lily pad in shades of green. Use light blue to shade the dress and then outline with a dark pencil. You could add a fish in the water.

Leave areas pale to show the light on the water

Autumn Fairy

1 Draw an oval above two overlapping bell shapes. Add guidelines to position the arms and legs.

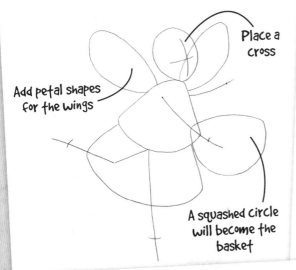

Place a cross

Add petal shapes for the wings

A squashed circle will become the basket

2 Draw a handle for the basket. Add triangles in the two bell shapes, which will help you form the dress.

Begin to shape the arms, hands and legs

Add the pointed neckline of her dress and the neck

Triangle shapes will become the leaves of the dress

Start to draw the feet

3 Start to shape the leaves of her dress. Use softer lines to shape the arms, hands, legs and feet.

Add the facial features

Begin to shape the wings

Draw circles in the basket for the fruit and berries

The Autumn Fairy is busy gathering fruits and berries to store for the winter!

4 Rub out the guidelines. Add the hair and hairband. Draw little lines of detail on the leaves of her dress.

There are two antennae on the hairband

Begin to add shading to her dress

You can add spots to her tights

Shade the basket and fruit

Use lots of little lines to show the texture of the hair. Make the lines curved so it does not look too neat.

5 Use lots of reds, oranges and browns to colour the autumn leaves of her dress. Shade the under layers darker.

Colour the fruit in red and gold and use purple for the blackberries

Winter Fairy

1 Draw an oval for the head with a smaller oval below it. Then add two overlapping bell shapes.

Add a cross to help you place the facial features

oblongs will form the arms

2 Add sharp, pointed shapes for the wings. Start to shape the arms and legs, using guidelines.

Add guidelines for the sleeves

Draw rough shapes for the hands

Begin to draw the skates

3 Shape the wings. If you make them slightly pointed they will look icy.

Draw the facial features

Add little lines for the fur of the sleeves and collar

Draw the hands

Shape the legs and skates

Divide the skirt into feather shapes

The Winter Fairy is an expert ice-skater and swooshes and swirls on the ice!

Every snowflake is different. Use a simple, star shape as a guide, then use the snowflakes on this page to help you create your own.

4 Add lots of detail and texture to the wings, feathers and fur. Begin to add shading.

Add a warm hat and a little hair escaping from underneath

Lots of little lines will show the feathers

5 Use pale blues or greys to add detail to the feathers and fur. Colour the wings in pale blue to make them look icy. The top, boots and hat could be red to contrast with the fluffy white fur and feathers.

Add some pale blue lines to show the ice

Baby Fairy

1 Draw a circle for the head. Then add a larger, squashed circle for the basket.

Remember when you draw a baby fairy that the face is rounder and the forehead is bigger than a more grown-up fairy's. Her wings are also smaller.

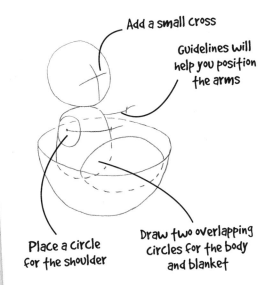

Add a small cross

Guidelines will help you position the arms

Place a circle for the shoulder

Draw two overlapping circles for the body and blanket

2 Start to roughly shape the arms and hands. Add the neck shape. A baby fairy's neck is a little fatter and shorter than a grown-up fairy's.

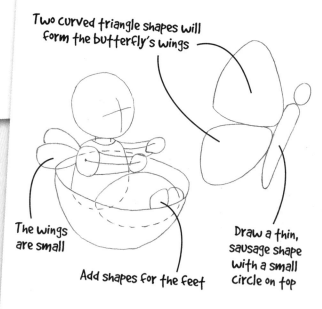

Two curved triangle shapes will form the butterfly's wings

The wings are small

Add shapes for the feet

Draw a thin, sausage shape with a small circle on top

Until this baby fairy's wings are strong enough to fly, she gets around in her butterfly basket!

3 Add the facial features. Use the guidelines to shape the arms, hands and feet. Begin to shape her top.

There is a hairband and a flower in her hair

She is laughing with her eyes closed

Start to draw the reins

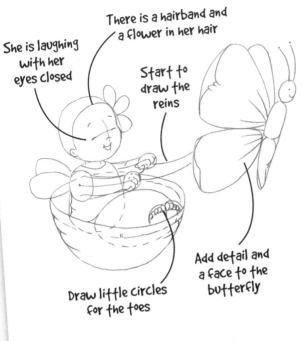

Draw little circles for the toes

Add detail and a face to the butterfly

4 Erase the guidelines. Add the hair and draw a few bits flicking back, to show movement. You can also add lines showing that she is flying through the air.

Shape the wings

Finish the reins

Shade the detail of the butterfly's wings

Little, wavy lines will add texture to the basket

Add spots to the blanket

5 Use pinks and purples for her top, flower, hairband and blanket. Leave white paper showing through for the spots. Colour the basket in different shades of brown for texture.

The wings are transparent, so you can see the basket through them

Fairy King

2 Draw the large wings. Add a wide, curved oblong above the head. Then draw two lines from its bottom corners to the shoulders.

Add a shape for the hand

This hand is resting on his hip

Begin to form the cape

Draw two triangles that meet in the middle of the body

1 Draw an oval for the head, overlapping a rectangle for the body. Add guidelines to position the arms and legs.

A circle will help you draw the elbow

Draw wide sleeves

Add the belt

Start to form the legs

Guidelines will help you draw the boots

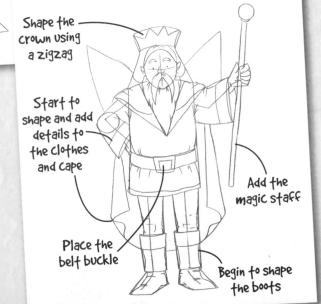

3 Add the facial features and ears. Draw two long, thin shapes under the nose for the moustache. From the bottom of the face, add the beard.

Shape the crown using a zigzag

Start to shape and add details to the clothes and cape

Add the magic staff

Place the belt buckle

Begin to shape the boots

4 Erase the guidelines. Then add detail to the crown, hair, beard and clothes.

Add some sparkly magic

Draw the details of the wings

He has a large ring

The Fairy King is very grand and he has a special staff to make powerful magic all over Fairyland!

5 Use rich, bright colours for the king's clothes. The inside of his cloak can be a different colour to the outside for contrast. You can add a pattern to his tunic. Add little lines in grey for the hair, leaving some places white.

Colour the boots black, leaving some areas white to show that they are shiny and to form buckles

Fairy Queen

1 Draw an oval for the head and a curved oblong on top for the crown. Add a cup shape for the torso and a large, bell shape for the skirt of her dress.

Add a cross

Draw the neck

Start to show the basic shapes of her clothes

Draw two lines from the waist for her cape

2 Draw a large oval behind your fairy for her throne, using the crown shape to guide you. Start to shape the neckline, necklace and clothes.

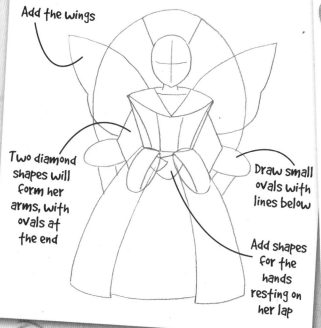

Add the wings

Two diamond shapes will form her arms, with ovals at the end

Draw small ovals with lines below

Add shapes for the hands resting on her lap

3 Draw the facial features, ears and earrings. Start to shape the crown and throne. Add detail to the clothes, necklace and hands.

Add a diamond to the necklace

Divide the ovals to make flower shapes

Small triangles show the tips of her shoes

Draw a line of fur on the cape

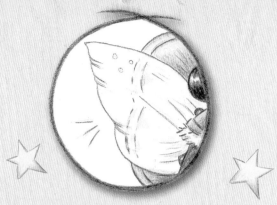

To show transparent wings, leave some white patches and show some yellow patches where the wings are in front of the throne. Add a broken line for the edge of the throne.

4 Erase the guidelines. Place jewel stones on the crown, necklace and cape. Add little, short lines to show the texture of the fur trim.

The wings are transparent

Add the hair

Sparkle lines

Draw fold lines

Add a ring

5 Use yellow and orange tones for anything gold. Colour the clothes with rich, bright colours. You can use lots of different colours for the jewel stones.

Leave small areas white on the jewel stones and add little lines to show how they sparkle!

The Fairy Queen is waiting to help fairies with broken spells and to give rewards to those who have been doing good deeds!

43

Gallery

THESE PAGES WILL GIVE YOU EXTRA INSPIRATION FOR YOUR PICTURES. HAVE A LOOK AT OTHER WAYS TO DRAW FAIRIES AND DIFFERENT THINGS YOU COULD ADD TO YOUR FAIRY SCENES.

Fairy people

Fairies can look just like little people with wings. You could try drawing your family and friends as fairies and then give them your pictures as cards and presents.

Fairy stories

These fairies are part of a scene, surrounded by flowers. You could put your fairies in scenes and create your own stories about what they are doing.

Sparkling fairies

You can draw lots of little stars to show that your fairies are sparkling.

45

Fox

Butterfly

Dragonfly

Butterflies and dragonflies have beautiful, delicate wings. They might help you to draw fairy wings.

Mouse

You could add mice to your fairy scenes to show the size of your fairies. Would they be any bigger than the mice?

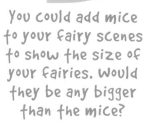
Rabbit

Robin

Practise drawing this robin or try to spot one. These beautiful birds could be added to a garden scene.

Frog

Toadstool

Fairy houses or seats could be made from a toadstool.

Clouds

You could draw white fluffy clouds behind your fairy to show how high she is flying.

Blackberries

Leaves

Autumn leaves will give you great ideas for fairy clothes. Look at their colour and texture for inspiration.

Conkers

Flowers

Look at petals to help you draw delicate fairy clothes.

First published in 2009 by Miles Kelly Publishing Ltd
Bardfield Centre, Great Bardfield, Essex, CM7 4SL, UK

Copyright © Miles Kelly Publishing Ltd 2009

2 4 6 8 10 9 7 5 3 1

EDITORIAL DIRECTOR Belinda Gallagher
ART DIRECTOR Jo Brewer
MANAGING EDITOR Rosie McGuire
ASSISTANT EDITOR Sarah Parkin
DESIGNER Michelle Cannatella
PRODUCTION MANAGER Elizabeth Brunwin
REPROGRAPHICS Anthony Cambray,
Stephan Davis, Jennifer Hunt
REPROGRAPHICS ASSISTANT Charlie Pearson

ISBN 978-1-84810-147-0

Printed in China

British Library Cataloguing-in-Publication Data
A catalogue record for this book is available from the British Library

ACKNOWLEDGEMENTS
The publishers would like to thank the following sources
for the use of their photographs:
Page 5 (glitter pens) Alison Bowden/Fotolia.com;
16–17 (background) deardone/Fotolia.com

All other images are from the Miles Kelly Archives

With thanks to the pupils at St Peter's C of E Primary School,
Coggeshall, for their help with this book

Made with paper from a sustainable forest

www.mileskelly.net
info@mileskelly.net

www.factsforprojects.com
The one-stop homework helper – pictures, facts, videos, projects and more